60+ ways to enrich a funeral

FINISHING
TOUCHES

BY JEAN FRANCIS

The Milestone Publishing Company.

The information address:

Jean Francis,
28 Depot Road,
Horsham,
West Sussex,
RH13 5HA.

www.pre-needfuneralplanning.co.uk

ISBN 978-0-9568234-0-3

Printed in Horsham, West Sussex.

Introduction

This book informs readers of the many choices available when planning their own funeral or that of a loved one. Such ideas enrich and personalise the occasion, in many cases at little or no extra cost.

Plan, talk and even laugh about your funeral arrangements with family and/or those close to you long before there is a need.

Planning and pre-paying for your own funeral can ease pressure on loved ones. Alternatively, part-plan and at least write down what you don't want.

Have you made a will, written a letter containing your final wishes and drawn up powers of attorney?

If so, does your next of kin know where to find these documents?

Consider making a video-recording that includes your memories and messages to leave for loved ones.

Gain awareness of environmental issues and the location of natural burial grounds in your area by visiting:

www.naturaldeath.org.uk

Will you choose cremation or burial? Informed choices will help with your decision making: 'The Good Funeral Guide' by Charles Cowling is an ideal starting point for your research:

ISBN 978-1-4411-5731-7

Consider choosing a green burial where a tree can be planted to mark the spot, instead of a gravestone. In time this will become a beautiful place for loved ones to visit, protected from developers and a haven for wildlife.

It is possible to be buried in your own garden or on private land. Should this idea appeal to you, visit:

www.naturaldeath.org.uk

Take into account the many choices of eco-friendly coffins available: sustainable pine, bamboo, cardboard, willow, sea-grass, water-hyacinth, wool, cane, and more.

Have you considered organ donation or leaving your body to medical science? This needs to be arranged in advance using the following link:

www.organdonation.nhs.uk/ukt

It is possible to pay your last respects to a loved one, spending time with them in the chapel of rest. An appointment should be made in advance with the funeral director.

Friends like to be helpful. Accept their offers: a meal, child care, order of service/ceremony sheets and help with baking, flowers and transport.

Planning the Funeral

When planning a funeral, create an occasion that reflects the character and values of the deceased. Consider adopting a theme.

Recommended reading: 'Time to Go: The Importance of Saying Goodbye:' by Jean Francis,

ISBN 0-595-31859-2

Locate a funeral director with an open attitude, willing to support families who wish to be individual and not conform to solemn tradition: 'The Natural Death Handbook' provides this information:

ISBN 978-1-907222-05-4

It is possible to arrange a private funeral, followed at a later date by a public memorial during which a life is truly celebrated.

Many people will of course contact their own religious leaders when arranging a funeral, honouring the age-old rituals and traditions of their own faith.

It is possible for a family member or close friend to conduct the service or ceremony.

Whether religious or not, spiritual ceremonies can be created and delivered according to family wishes by Interfaith ministers (who are members of the Interfaith Foundation).

www.interfaithfoundation.org

An independent celebrant will spend time with the family to create a ceremony that reflects the personal beliefs and philosophies of the deceased. This can be religious or non-religious, or a fusion of the two, visit:

www.pre-needfuneralplanning.co.uk

For those preferring a totally secular send-off, a humanist ceremony may be more appropriate, visit:

www.humanism.org.uk

A civil funeral ceremony is basically secular, but should the family wish to include a favourite hymn or reading, this is fine; visit:

www.iocf.org.uk

If cremation is chosen, consider booking extra time at the crematorium to avoid feeling rushed.

At the moment of departure from the crematorium, the curtains may be left open around the coffin if preferred. Alternatively the coffin can remain on trestles throughout.

A funeral ceremony can take place not only in a church, crematorium or by the graveside, but for instance at home, in the garden, the local pub or in a hired hall.

For a more celebratory occasion ask friends not to wear black and for the funeral directors to wear colourful ties.

The Journey

Hire a bus to carry the coffin and the mourners through busy streets, avoiding stress and parking problems.

Transport the casket on a decorated horse-drawn farm cart and have friends travel with it.

For a grand farewell, hire a Victorian-style horse-drawn hearse to carry the coffin.

For a keen biker, transport the casket in a motor-cycle hearse.

A hand-pulled cart can be used to carry the coffin to its resting place. Within the procession of people consider including family dogs, on leads of course.

For a keen dancer, have a band to lead a procession of family and friends to the funeral; some may even dance to the music.

The family could personalise a cardboard coffin with messages, photographs and symbols, using water-based glues, paints, stickers and felt-tipped pens.

Cover a natural pine coffin with a beautiful quilt or a flag that can be removed after the service/ceremony.

Dress the deceased in their favourite clothes, preferably those made of natural fabrics.

Think about placing photographs and love-letters in the coffin and, - at whatever age - a cuddly toy made of and stuffed with natural materials of course.

Write a letter to the deceased, especially if there are unresolved issues.

Have family members and friends act as bearers to carry the coffin.

As an alternative to a wreath or spray, weave flowers and herbs into a coffin, such as one made of willow.

Combine a floral tribute with the loved one's hobby or interest: a favourite hat, daily newspaper or a can of lager, imagination being the only limitation.

If flowers are to be taken to a care home or hospice after the funeral, when placing the order ask the florist to supply posies or hand-tied bunches rather than wreaths.

Suggest that instead of floral tributes, mourners bring a single bloom to place on the coffin and make donations to a nominated charity.

The Ceremony

When writing a eulogy, honour the person by remembering them just as they were.

Personalise the order of service sheet by including a photograph of the deceased.

Select music, poetry and readings that are personally meaningful and reflect the loved one's life; even telling a few jokes can be appropriate.

Leave a space in the ceremony for private contemplation and for friends who may wish to contribute a few words.

Prepare a commemorative presentation of photographs and/or a video to project during the service/ceremony or afterwards.

Drink a toast to the memory of the deceased during the ceremony, if permitted.

Live music can bring an added dimension to the occasion.

Encourage a grandchild to write and read a poem that they have written about a grandparent. This can help them mourn their loss.

End the service/ceremony on a light note that people will remember and take away with them.

Invite people to sign a special book or cards with their personal memories of the deceased.

Have a container available in which to collect donations for a chosen charity in memory of the deceased.

Resting Place

Consider lining the grave with leaves, fleece, hay or straw to give a cosy appearance.

For retired servicemen and women arrange for a bugler to play 'The Last Post'.

For a Scottish flavour, hire a Highland Piper in full ceremonial dress to lead the procession and play at the graveside.

For the comfort of mourners, erect a gazebo at the graveside to afford shelter from the elements.

In Memory

The floral tribute from the coffin can be used as a table decoration for the gathering that follows, perhaps with a photograph of the deceased placed beside it.

Organise a shared meal, a picnic, bake family favourites; or if the deceased's favourite food happened to be fish and chips or hog roast, why not honour the fact?

Release bio-degradable balloons with labels attached on which messages of remembrance have been written.

Why not fly kites and watch them rise into the freedom of the sky, representing the freeing of the spirit?

Release a pair of white doves as a symbol of peace and watch them soar.

At a funeral in early spring, give each mourner a pot of snowdrops as a token of new life.

A small tree on a grave decorated with wild bird food makes a lovely tribute at Christmas instead of flowers.

Remember the anniversary each year by lighting a candle.

There are numerous ways of using cremated ashes as lasting and imaginative memorials. These and many more ideas will be outlined in other books in this series.

For further information and ideas, visit:

www.pre-needfuneralplanning.co.uk